A loving grandmother ca
ter, Faith. And she sees
tions with her own careg
vulnerable places in our
our own walk with our Creator. We rejoice as Faith thrives in the
unmeasured care of her grandmother, and perhaps we begin to
understand the gifts that we have received in this mysterious dance
of life. Brew a lovely cup of tea and settle down for a rich experience
with *Tiny Gifts.*

—Lyn Holley Doucet
Author, *Healing Troubled Hearts, Light on a River's Turning:
Meditations on the Life of Hildegard of Bingen,* and Other Titles

This outstanding book should be in every NICU in every hospital. Experiencing the vulnerability of a premature infant creates
a mutual vulnerability that leads to understanding some of life's
greatest lessons. Sandra Smith has woven her deep spiritual insights
into this enlightening testimony of faith.

—Victoria S. Schmidt
Executive Director, Theresians International, Co-Author of
Three Books, e.g. *Soul Light for the Dark Night, Daily Meditations
on Healing from Trauma and Abuse,* Gentle Path Press, 2019

Through this grandmother's love, reflections, and written word,
the reader is invited to celebrate, deepen, and refresh our faith.
Aware and in awe of the actions and development of her granddaughter, Faith, a newborn preemie, Sandra invites us to our own
growing up to God. She is confessional, honest, and authentic in
naming her spiritual struggles and calls herself and others to move
toward God while embracing imperfection. With her wisdom and
insight as educator, spiritual director, and now as grandmother, she
invites us to laugh, to love, and to have faith.

—The Reverend Dr. Tim P. VanDuivendyk
Minister, Hospital Chaplain, Licensed Professional
Counselor, Licensed Marriage and Family Therapist,
and Author of *The Unwanted Gift of Grief*

ISBN 978-1-63630-338-3 (Paperback)
ISBN 978-1-63630-339-0 (Digital)

Covenant Books, Inc.
11661 Hwy 707
Murrells Inlet, SC 29576
www.covenantbooks.com

Tiny Gifts

Faith Lessons from a Preemie

Sandra Smith

Dedicated to my precious granddaughter,
Faith, who continues to inspire me!

CONTENTS

Acknowledgments

To MY FAMILY AND ESPECIALLY my husband of more than fifty years. You are all my rock.

To John Faulk, senior writer at the Christian Broadcasting Network, whose invaluable advice and editing skills breathed life into this devotional.

To Theresians International, Inc., and especially to my Reflections Community. You were with me from the beginning and have prayed and supported me in all my endeavors.

To Tina, my assistant publisher, and all the family of Covenant Books who made this devotional a reality.

But most importantly, to my Creator and LORD who guided me every step of the way!

Born Too Soon

FAITH WAS BORN TOO SOON. At only thirty-three weeks, her little lungs were not ready to be weaned from the womb. As a result, she spent three weeks in the NICU with tubes and needles extending from every orifice of her body. It was heartbreaking to see this tiny being weighing less than four pounds lying inert, the result of a drug-induced coma. The mechanical sound of her breathing machine was the only indication of life. I cried every time I saw her. But through the power of prayer and the incessant knocking at God's door to heal this little body, she improved. Despite the doctor's prognosis that she would need to remain in the hospital for two months, she was at home in her own crib within three weeks!

What a joy to see her, tiny as she was, breathing and crying and behaving as any other newborn. And what a testament to the goodness of God and the power of prayer! I have always believed that through prayer, God can usher in miracles and turn tragedy into joy. Faith, our miracle granddaughter, became not only my witness to the mercy and kindness of God, but she became my teacher. Through the day-to-day care of this preemie, God fueled my soul with new insights and a deeper awareness of His abundant love for all His children!

Both of our life's lessons began the day Faith was born!

Therefore I tell you, all that you ask for in prayer, believe that you will receive it and it shall be yours. (Mark 11:24)

Pure Drop of Heaven

OFTEN WHEN I HELD FAITH, she would gaze at a spot just above my head, her expressive eyes moving back and forth as though watching a scene playing out above me. It is said that babies at this young age can actually see the aura of a person. They can be entertained with the vivid colors emanating from the energy of a living being. I believe this phenomenon is real and wondered if Faith saw angels flying about. For her, the supernatural world would be natural. Faith, a pure drop from heaven and newly arrived on this earth, would find it easy and commonplace to commune with the angels hovering over us humans—protecting, guiding, and praying for us.

We all arrive on this earth fresh from our communion with all that is on the other side. As the French philosopher, Pierre Teilhard de Chardin, stated, "We are not humans having a spiritual journey, but rather we are all spiritual beings having an earthly experience." Unfortunately, as I age, my memories of the supernatural dim, no longer remaining in my consciousness. But it is wonderful to realize that, like Faith, I once existed in a state of purity, unspoiled by my physicality and able to commune with supernatural creatures! At one time, I was completely content, blissfully happy, and free from all discomfort. Now, when my body feels physical or emotional pain, I can close my eyes and try to recapture the memory of a time when I was totally free and saturated in the joy of communing with the angels!

Before I formed you in the womb I knew you, before you were born I dedicated you. (Jeremiah 1:5)

[A]s we look not to what is seen but to what is unseen; for what is seen is transitory, but what is unseen is eternal. (2 Corinthians 4:18)

Demanding

As a tiny baby, Faith would scream hysterically when she felt hungry as if she feared she would not be fed. Her anger and agitation would escalate into a frenzied state. She never seemed to remember that the last time she was hungry, her needs were promptly met with a warm breast or bottle. Instead, she wailed impatiently and inconsolably.

Unlike Faith, my God never demands anything from me. Rather, He invites me in a gentle, loving way to trust Him and allow Him to be the Lord of my life. His voice is a persistent, quiet nudging within my spirit—a tiny whisper that beckons me to walk daily in His path and to surrender myself completely to His will.

Yet, contrary to Jesus's example, when I have a need, I often become the screaming infant who demands that my cries be promptly heard and addressed. The slightest delay in receiving an answer to prayer leads to frustration and doubt. My memory lapses, and I fail to recall that Jesus is a faithful God who *always* hears my cries and answers me. Sometimes the answers come in ways I did not anticipate. Frequently, He asks me to wait upon Him and allow His perfect timing to be accomplished. It is at these times that I must put aside my impatience and doubts and cling to Him in trust and obedience. God will never fail to respond to me but will always provide exactly what I need to satisfy the longings of my heart and nourish my soul.

Trust in the LORD with all your heart, on your own intelligence do not rely. (Proverbs 3:5)

Commit your way to the LORD; trust in him and he will act. (Psalm 37:5)

Foot-Washing

ONE MORNING, I WAS GIVING Faith a bath, a daily event we both enjoyed. As she lay in the tub on her sponge mat, I lifted one foot, kissed it, and lathered it with soap. As I gently washed that tiny foot, I was overcome with an unexpected feeling of pure joy. How I loved that foot and that tiny body! Feeling the smoothness of her newborn skin, counting those small sausage toes, and caressing the shape and curve of that foot filled me with such gratitude and love that tears sprang from my eyes.

Suddenly, I recalled another foot-washing scenario. On Holy Thursday, Jesus removed His tunic, tied it around His waist, and knelt in front of His beloved disciples to wash their feet. As He intimately held the calloused and dirty foot of each disciple, I am sure He felt the same sense of love and reverence as I experienced when I held Faith's foot. How He loved those men!

Was this foot-washing event more than just a lesson in servitude? Could it be that Jesus used this servant's task to bless and comfort Himself? Nothing could have given Him more joy than to embrace and caress the foot of a person He loved unconditionally. Perhaps sharing this love and companionship with each disciple in the intimate act of washing their feet provided Him with the strength and resolve to continue His journey to the cross.

Meditating upon this scene gives me a greater insight into the unconditional love of my Savior, and I am humbled and in awe of this magnificent yet simple gesture of reverencing one another.

But God proves his love for us in that while we were still sinners Christ died for us. (Romans 5:8)

Beloved, let us love one another, because love is of God; everyone who loves is begotten by God and knows God. (1 John 4:7)

Poop and Other Messes

BABIES MAKE MESSES. THEY POOP, spit up, and generally require several changes of clothing in a single day. But even when I needed to clean the poop, change the clothes, or wipe a runny nose, I never stopped loving that precious child; nor did I, even during her growing years, ever demand that she "clean up her act!"

Grownups are no different. I, too, make messes, some more smelly than others, but God never stops loving me. He simply lifts me up, wipes clean my mistakes, perfumes me with the oil of forgiveness, and reminds me there is nothing I can ever do to separate me from His love. This abundant love removes all shame, is transforming, and gives me the courage to pick myself back up and try again. What a good and gracious Father I have—one who never condemns and never gives up on helping me to grow

in grace and holiness, no matter how many messes
I create!

*For I am convinced that neither death, nor
life, nor angels, nor principalities, nor present things, nor future things, nor powers, nor
height, nor depth, nor any other creature will
be able to separate us from the love of God in
Christ Jesus our Lord. (Romans 8:38–39)*

*But you have mercy on all, because you can
do all things; and you overlook sins for the
sake of repentance. (Wisdom 11:23)*

Sounds

BABIES ARE VERY NOISY CREATURES. Even in sleep, they are not completely quiet. Faith's cries, laughter, coos, and babbles were beautiful background music to my everyday life. By actively listening, I quickly learned to decipher the meaning of each precious sound and could respond accordingly.

Listening is an integral part of my everyday world. Through sounds, I perceive life. I hear the ordinariness of my day through the ringing of the telephone, the cacophony of city traffic, or the clanking of dinnerware at mealtimes. I resonate with the sounds of nature, the cries of birds in flight, the whishing of the wind, the rustle of flora, the chirping of crickets, and the whispers of night creatures. I listen to the peals of lightning and thunder and the drops of rain beating against my windowpane.

When I listen, I hear the voices of loved ones offering words of affirmation, instruction, warning, conversation. I feel connected when I hear the laughter, anger, tears, and songs of others. I listen for the calling of my name from a family member summoning my help, a friend seeking companionship, or the birthday song sung in my honor. I hear my body speak through the beating of my heart, the growling of a hungry stomach, or the creaking of joints stiff with age, and I give thanks for being alive. I am blessed when I listen to the words of Scripture and the prayers of my church congregation. Even in the dark, I listen to the silence and feel at peace.

Every breath, whisper, or noise I perceive is an indication of life happening all around me. Where there is life, there is God. God embodies every sound that I hear. When I stop and listen to the sounds of my world, I hear the voice of God, and I am in awe.

Keep on doing what you have learned and received and heard and seen in me. Then the God of peace will be with you. (Philippians 4:9)

The wise by hearing them will advance in learning, the intelligent will gain sound guidance. (Proverbs 1:5)

Whoever has ears ought to hear. (Matthew 11:15)

Gazing Upon My Face

WHEN FAITH BEGAN TO OPEN her eyes and focus, she would often stare intently at me. It was as if she were studying every feature of my face to imprint it upon her memory. Her eyes would never waver from their concentrated gaze, and I would find myself captured by the intensity of her look. Like a swirl of water spiraling downward, Faith drew me into her deep blue recesses where I was content to languish.

Jesus also knows my face. He has created me from clay and sculptured every feature. He has memorized the curve of my cheek, the angle of my nose, the color of my eyes. He sees every wrinkle, mole, and freckle lining my face. He has numbered every hair on my head. Like Faith, He is content just to look, making no judgments or demands upon me. His only request is that I, in turn, behold His face.

Gazing silently into the eyes of Jesus through meditation, prayer, and Scripture opens my spirit to perceive not only His goodness and beauty but to recognize in Him the image of the Father. As Jesus proclaimed in His word, "When you see me, you see the Father" (John 14:9). To see the Father is to see love without boundaries and mercy without limits. Through the Father's probing gaze, the darkest recesses of my soul are illuminated, and I am transformed. My Father's gaze is upon me continuously. I only need to glance in His direction, and I will be captured by the look of unconditional love—the same look I recognized in the eyes of a newborn!

[W]hile keeping our eyes fixed on Jesus, the leader and perfecter of faith. (Hebrews 12:2)

One thing I ask of the LORD; this I seek: To dwell in the LORD's house all the days of my life, To gaze on the LORD's beauty, to visit his temple. (Psalm 27:4)

Swaddling

As a newborn baby, I would swaddle Faith in her comfy receiving blanket. Snugly wrapped, she was soothed and able to sleep more deeply.

The Gospel of Luke tells us that Jesus was also swaddled while He lay in a manger (Luke 2:7). Perhaps this was the first indication that we are all made to be swaddled. Since my conception, I have been wrapped in God-given cloths of love, protection, grace, mercy, compassion, and acceptance. These are the bindings that provide peace and security while cradled in the arms of my Creator.

But at times, I have chosen to be wrapped in harmful strips. Sinful bands of pride, shame, unforgiveness, fear, unkindness, envy, or anger wind themselves tightly about my spirit and act as a barrier to God's life-giving grace. Bindings of this nature lead to the tomb. But my merciful God is not content to leave me there. He commands me, as He did with the biblical Lazarus who was bound head to foot, to "come out" (John 11:43). He further demands that I be untied. With repentance, my bindings are loosened, and I am set free—free to once again be swaddled in God's compassionate love.

I will rejoice heartily in the LORD, my being exults in my God; For he has clothed me with garments of salvation, and wrapped me in a robe of justice. (Isaiah 61:10)

I will give you the keys to the kingdom of heaven. "Whatever you bind on earth shall be bound in heaven; and whatever you loose on earth shall be loosed in heaven." (Matthew 16:19)

Do not let love and fidelity forsake you; bind them around your neck; write them on the tablet of your heart. Then will you win favor and esteem before God and human beings. (Proverbs 3:3–4)

Binkies

FAITH LOVED HER BINKY. SHE was never without that pacifier, especially at bedtime. Her binky provided comfort and a sense of security in her young life. She clung to that pacifier well into her late toddler years.

I often ask myself, "What am I clinging to?" Is there anything so central to my life that I would feel devastated without it? Anything that takes priority over God in my heart is essentially an idol. What have become my idols that crowd out the love of Jesus?

Even good things, such as writing, speaking, and being a grandmother can become overwhelmingly important to me. Then Jesus nudges me with a gentle reminder that my sense of security, rightfulness, and balance can come only from Him. Putting other things before Him, regardless of how wonderful they seem, will eventually stunt my spiritual growth. Just as Faith needed to grow up and sacrifice her pacifier,

I, too, need to let go of anything that takes priority over my God.

While I will continue to use and celebrate the gifts that God gave me, I will ask for the grace to keep these gifts from becoming my sole source of strength and comfort.

I will seek to make God my only Binky!

A clean heart create for me, God; renew within me a steadfast spirit. (Psalm 51:12)

You shall not have other gods beside me. (Exodus 20:3)

Projectiles

FAITH'S EARLY ARRIVAL RESULTED IN an immature digestive system. It was always a challenge to feed her. Regardless of how slowly she was fed the bottle, the contents would inevitably spew out in a projectile of regurgitated milk, soaking everything in its path. I never gave her a bottle without a supply of towels at hand; one to cover her, one for myself, and others to safeguard nearby furniture. Everything needed protection from the explosion sure to follow.

Every day I face projectiles of a supernatural nature. When the enemy maliciously slings darts at me while I strive to live out my Gospel values, God provides me with His Living Word as my defense. Scripture commands me to wear the armor of salvation, use justice as my breastplate, and to place the belt of truth around my waist. Additionally, I am given the shield of faith which covers and strengthens me when storms threaten to weaken my spirit.

Daily, I am equipped with everything necessary to thwart the tactics of the devil—God's love, His promises, and His faithful presence. I am girded with the courage and strength to "fight the good fight," as admonished by St. Paul in his letter to Timothy (1 Timothy 1:18). Just as I took all precautions to keep Faith dry and comfortable, God lovingly ensures my safety with His constant shield of protection.

In all circumstances, hold faith as a shield, to quench all [the] flaming arrows of the evil one. (Ephesians 6:16)

Every weapon fashioned against you shall fail. (Isaiah 54:17)

Storms

THE THUNDER DEAFENED THE NIGHT! As the storm raged, I worried that Faith would be startled awake by the ferocity of the rain pelting against her bedroom window and the deafening *boom* of the angry clouds ramming into one another. But undisturbed, she slept well, like a baby!

What a gift! I thought as I watched her contentedly sleep. When the storms in my life crash about me, seldom do I let go and rest without disturbance. More likely, I act like the panicked disciples in the sinking boat who roughly awaken Jesus, crying, "Help! We're drowning" (Mark 4:38)!

A priest friend of mine always preached that when the storms of our lives threaten to sink us, we simply ask Jesus not to calm the storm but to get in the boat with us. After watching Faith in her quiet slumber, I am prompted to go one step further.

I ask for the grace to quiet my fears, curl up to the napping Jesus, and rest peacefully while the storm rages on. What better way to say, "Jesus, I trust in you!"

[W]hen I am afraid, in you I place my trust. (Psalm 56:4)

For over all, his glory will be shelter and protection: shade from the parching heat of day, refuge and cover from storm and rain. (Isaiah 4:6)

Lammy

FAITH'S FAVORITE TOY AS A baby was a small stuffed lamb. This wooly creature with a sweet smile stitched on its face provided instant comfort for our new grandbaby. When you pressed the paw, the lamb played a soft lullaby while gently swinging its head side to side. Faith was mesmerized by the sight and sound of this inanimate creature and would stare at it intently until her eyelids became heavy with sleep.

As I sat cradling this stuffed toy, I was reminded how often in Scripture we are called sheep. Jesus refers to us as His flock, and He is the Good Shepherd. A shepherd knows how helpless his sheep are against the attacks of wolves. When threatened, their only defense is to huddle together with the herd or to try to outrun their attacker.

If Jesus calls me His sheep, then He is aware of my vulnerabilities. He knows that I am not equipped to fight my battles alone, but rather, I was designed to be totally dependent on Him for guidance, protection, and care. As my Shepherd, He uses His staff to steer me in the direction I need to go, and He places His rod between me and my enemies, shielding me from harm. He provides me with a flock of believers who support and uphold my faith in times of distress, so I am never alone.

My Good Shepherd is ever vigilant, ever present. When threatened by predators, my greatest defense is to run quickly to Him, hide behind His robe, and trust that He will defend me from all harm. I can proclaim with conviction the words uttered by King David in Psalm 23, "The LORD is my Shepherd, I shall not want." As a loved sheep in His flock, all my fears and anxieties give way to a calm and quiet confidence in His care.

*For thus says the L*ORD *GOD: Look! I myself will search for my sheep and examine them. (Ezekiel 34:11)*

I am the good shepherd. A good shepherd lays down his life for the sheep. (John 10:11)

Change on a Dime

BABIES ARE FICKLE CREATURES. THEY can be exceedingly happy and content one moment, only to dissolve into hysterical tears the next. Whether it is hunger, a need to sleep, an unexpected bump, or a myriad of other reasons, a baby's world can change instantly from calm and serene to a tsunami of tears, wails, and inconsolability.

As an adult, my path seems to follow the same zigzag trajectory of emotions. When all in my world is comfortable, I am serene, happy, and satisfied. But as soon as the apple cart is tipped in the opposite direction, my peace flies out the window. While I may not always dissolve into uncontrollable tears, my soul begins to rage against the injustices I perceive have befallen me. Plagued with doubts about God's love for me, I clench my fists and ask, "Why?"

These periods of unhappiness completely cloud my memories of the countless times I have experienced consolation and blessings. I forget that the desert will soon bloom again, and peace and joy will return. But most importantly, I fail to remember that when the soul cries out to God in the deepest moments of longing, profound grace is imminent, and my spirit will once again rejoice in the mercy and goodness of my Creator.

The wilderness and the parched land will exult; the Arabah will rejoice and bloom; Like the crocus it shall bloom abundantly, and rejoice with joyful song. (Isaiah 35:1–2)

[B]ecause of the tender mercy of our God by which the daybreak from on high will visit us to shine on those who sit in darkness and death's shadow, to guide our feet into the path of peace. (Luke 1:78–79)

Midnight Feedings

ON THE RARE OCCASIONS WHEN I would keep Faith overnight, midnight feedings became the favorite time of my day. As she contently sucked on her bottle, the world slowed and dimmed. All my concerns and worries also seemed to evaporate. I focused only on the present moment, sitting and rocking with my infant granddaughter in the stillness of the night. Those simple but priceless moments filled me with incredible peace and joy.

All the LORD asks of me is to sit with Him, focus only on the present moment, and allow the chaos of my mind to still and fade. No words need to be said, yet volumes are being spoken during those silent times. In fact, the silence is pregnant with the voice of God. Rumi, the poet and theologian, observes that "silence is God's language; everything else is a poor translation."

As I sit in quiet contemplation with my God, listening only for the soft whisperings of the Spirit, I am nourished with His presence and filled with the same joy and contentment as I experienced during those precious midnight feedings.

Be still and know that I am God! I am exalted among the nations, exalted on the earth. (Psalm 46:11)

Rather, I have stilled my soul, Like a weaned child to its mother, weaned is my soul. (Psalm 131:2)

Teething

TEETHING FOR A YOUNG CHILD can be brutal. Swollen gums, fever, and pain cause considerable discomfort for a little one. It was difficult to wait and watch with Faith as she experienced this necessary part of growing up. But once those teeth break through, a whole new and necessary chapter of a child's life begins. Teeth allow for natural chewing of solid foods. They also aid in speech development and affect a child's smile, self-confidence, and social skills.

As I grow in my spirituality, I, too, must cut new teeth. And like any teething child, I often experience pain, tears, and crankiness. I wail, "Why are you putting me through this, God? It hurts!" But God knows that growth is necessary and can only come from having gone through the fire. God is not content to leave me in the milk teeth stage, but rather, He knows that the next level of development will strengthen my relationship with Him. God always desires the "more" for me. The more "teeth" I develop, the better equipped I am to experience the deeper, meatier side of His grace and mercy.

Yes, spiritual growth can be as painful as the stages of physical development. But the pain is short-lived and the strength that ensues from suffering equips me for a brighter future—as bright as a child's tooth-filled smile!

The God of all grace who called you to his eternal glory through Christ [Jesus] will himself restore, confirm, strengthen, and establish you after you have suffered a little. (1 Peter 5:10)

Not only that, but we even boast of our afflictions, knowing that affliction produces endurance, and endurance, proven character, and proven character, hope. (Romans 5:3–4)

Brothers, I could not talk to you as spiritual people, but as fleshly people, as infants in Christ. I fed you milk, not solid food, because you were unable to take it. (1 Corinthians 3:1–2)

Dance of Life

ONE OF FAITH'S FAVORITE AMUSEMENTS was dancing. Even before she could walk, whenever she heard music, she would grab the nearest piece of furniture, pull herself erect, and bounce up and down to the beat of the music. Her entire body would wiggle as she performed her "happy" dance.

My own spiritual dance experience occurred during the season of Lent. Maybe the solemnity of that liturgical time of year weighed heavily on my mind as I sat at a red light and glumly watched one of those silly air-pumped balloon characters used by businesses to attract customers. As I observed this creature flailing about and twisting in all directions, I sullenly thought how its actions were a perfect example of the way life treats us! It jerks us around, and every time we try to stand up straight, we get jabbed in the stomach, doubling us over. Or an unexpected whammy from behind shifts our center of gravity, causing us to tumble head over heels. Life can be so unpredictable, continually throwing us off balance so we can never quite right ourselves.

Were the crazed movements of this inflatable balloon a depiction of my own inner turmoil? As the traffic light turned green, I unexpectedly realized the truth. Those frenetic gyrations were not irrational actions. They were the rhythmic movements of an energetic dance. With arms twirling merrily about and a silly grin plastered on its balloon face, this creature's body seemed to vibrate with enthusiasm and motivation. This was a celebration of life embraced and enjoyed with abandon. In that Easter moment, I knew I had two choices—either live my life as a constant struggle or fall into the arms of my risen Savior and joyously dance!

There is an appointed time for everything and a time for every affair under the heavens… A time to weep, and a time to laugh; a time to mourn, and a time to dance. (Ecclesiastes 3:1,4)

You changed my mourning into dancing; you took off my sackcloth and clothed me with gladness. (Psalm 30:12)

First Words

WHEN FAITH BEGAN TO DEVELOP speech, it became a challenge to teach her to say recognizable words. "Say Dada. Say Mama," I coached. Every day, I would repeat words to her until she uttered that first discernable word.

What words do I repeat to myself daily? What words does God speak to me to teach me in my spiritual development? Henri Nouwen, a Dutch Catholic priest and author, writes that we have an inner space that is profoundly affected by the repetition of words. He further states that our "inner room" is like a holy space that we need to decorate and keep in good order.

What phrases do I use to adorn my inner space? Do I listen and reiterate the loving words that God speaks to me every day, such as "You are My beloved in whom I delight"? More often, though, I dwell on negative self-talk. "I can't do this… I'm not worthy!"

It takes effort to silence the negativity and repeat uplifting words of affirmation, such as, "I am beautifully and wonderfully made" or "I can do all things through Christ Jesus who strengthens me." These words create a holy space within my inner sanctum, allowing the light of God to shine through the windows of my soul. Through prayer and repetition of the Holy Scriptures, I paint my inner wall with colors of hope and light that give evidence of the Spirit dwelling within. With continued practice, I can banish the negative statements of the inner critic from my vocabulary and verbalize only God's language of truth and love!

Let the words of my mouth be acceptable, the thoughts of my heart before you, LORD, my rock and my redeemer. (Psalm 19:15)

It is the spirit that gives life, while the flesh is of no avail. The words I have spoken to you are spirit and life. (John 6:63)

Strange Bedfellows

As a toddler, Faith instantly disliked Santa Claus! During the annual mall Christmas photo, she screamed bloody murder when placed on the lap of this bearded, red-suited stranger. Despite a generous amount of coaxing, she could not understand that this character represented happy times, wonderful surprises, and Christmas cheer. Even the offer of a candy cane could not convince her. Santa was not a familiar figure in her tiny world, and she let me know so with loud protests!

Looking back on my life, I can relate. I can even image how I would have felt if I had encountered biblical characters such as John the Baptist. What a strange creature! In his sackcloth, camel hair tunic, and his unappetizing diet of honey and locust, I would have instantly regarded him with suspicion and contempt—someone to avoid! I would have turned deaf ears to this unkempt, eccentric man's message. And yet, my rash judgment of John would have robbed me of a magnificent encounter with the divine. By scorning John the Baptist, I would not have witnessed Jesus's baptism nor would I have experienced the awe and majesty of the heavens parting while a dove descended upon Him. I would have deeply regretted the lost opportunity to hear the voice of God declaring that Jesus was His Son.

How many of God's messengers have I disregarded in my own life? How many people, even among my own family, have I dismissed as unworthy, simply because they do not look, speak, or think as I do? Could some of these people actually be harbingers of God's Word for my own spiritual growth? If God could use an odd person such as John the Baptist to announce the divinity of His Son, then perhaps I need to temper my critical judgments of others and be open to hearing the voice of God, regardless of how the message is packaged.

Therefore, do not make any judgment before the appointed time, until the LORD comes, for he will bring to light what is hidden in darkness and will manifest the motives of our hearts, and then everyone will receive praise from God. (1 Corinthians 4:5)

There is one lawgiver and judge who is able to save or to destroy. Who then are you to judge your neighbor? (James 4:12)

Birthday Party

A BIG CELEBRATION WAS PLANNED for Faith's first birthday. Everyone present rejoiced at the progress of this premature baby who was developmentally on track despite her fragile beginning. As part of the celebration, she was presented with her very own small birthday cake. When it was placed in front of her with a crowd of onlookers cheering her on, she seemed confused and not sure how to respond. Tentatively, Faith stuck one small finger in the icing and licked it but seemed unwilling to delve into the whole cake with gusto. Even with much prodding, she would not take more than a few cautious bites.

Every day, I celebrate a "birthday." I am born anew each morning with the prospects of good things to come. My day is wrapped in countless blessings, but like Faith, I am tentative about delving in. With my human frailties and limitations, I too often get caught up in the problems and uncertainties of life. I struggle with trusting a God who sometimes seems distant and unresponsive. I forget that God is a God of plenty and wants nothing more than to bless me in abundance.

There is an old folktale that states after we die, God will show us a whole room of unopened presents. Each present represents a gift or blessing that we did not unwrap. Do I want to waste all those blessings? Or would I prefer to be bold and ask for the grace to open my heart to the gifts that accompany every aspect of my life? A gifted life is a life worth celebrating! And that's the icing on the cake!

Put me to the test, says the LORD of hosts, And see if I do not open the floodgates of heaven for you, and pour down upon you blessing without measure! (Malachi 3:10)

The LORD will open up for you his rich storehouse, the heavens, to give your land rain in due season and to bless all the works of your hands. (Deuteronomy 28:12)

Trust Me

WHEN FAITH FIRST BEGAN TO walk, she would strike out on her wobbly legs toward me and throw herself into my arms. One day, a game ensued between me and her other grandmother. Standing between us as we sat on the floor, she would totter toward one grandmother, fall into her arms, and then repeat this process toward the other grandmother. She was extremely unsteady on her feet and would have fallen if we were not there to catch her each time. Undaunted, she continued her shaky treks across the room, totally trusting that she would be safe as she stumbled into our arms.

Aren't my actions the same with my God? I often say, "I'll do it myself" and then strike out on shaky legs. Like a tottering infant, I can be stubborn, independent, and hesitant to take those first tentative steps toward trusting my God. I stumble, lose my balance, and would come crashing down if God were not there to catch me. And catch me He does!

Throughout Jesus's entire life, He supported and encouraged those who struggled to reach Him. He caught Peter who fell while trying to walk on water. He gathered countless sinners in His arms of forgiveness, and He held and healed all the sufferings of those who cried out to Him. His mercy and compassion knew no limits and left little doubt that He could be trusted.

Faith never doubted that she would be secure in her grandmothers' arms. Could I not take a lesson from a determined toddler and simply trust that I, too, will be caught in my Father's embrace whenever I step out in faith?

He will not allow your foot to slip; or your guardian to sleep. (Psalm 121:3)

Blessed are those who trust in the LORD; the LORD will be their trust. (Jeremiah 17:7)

The Magi's Star

DURING THE CHRISTMAS SEASON, I often read the Nativity story to Faith. She especially enjoyed a children's book describing the animals in the stable gathered around the Baby Jesus. The story of the bright star that the Magi followed also captured her attention.

Both these stories so beautifully illustrate my own experiences of pursuing the newborn Savior. Sometimes I must be still and wait like the animals who were already in the stable when Mary gave birth to Jesus. They did not need to seek, but rather, Jesus came to them. How many times does He meet me in my everyday life without any effort on my part? The Magi, however, undertook a long and arduous journey relying upon a star to guide them.

In my daily pursuit of Jesus, I find myself asking, "What is my star?" What is the person, event, or object looming brightly in my life that may be guiding me to my Savior? Even my problems or worries may be stars that ultimately lead me closer to Jesus, prompting me to fall on my knees in homage to Him.

Each day, I pray the LORD will guide me with my own unique star. Whatever its form, I strive to follow it with the same eagerness and intensity as the wandering Magi. I, too, believe it will lead me to something astounding!

And your ears shall hear a word behind you: "This is the way; walk in it," when you would turn to the right or the left. (Isaiah 30:21)

Then the LORD will guide you always. (Isaiah 58:11)

After their audience with the king they set out. And behold, the star that they had seen at its rising preceded them, until it came and stopped over the place where the child was. (Matthew 2:9)

Sit Down and Scoot

As a wobbly tot, Faith was unsure of how to traverse the small step down into our family room. That two-inch drop was a major obstacle in her forward motion. Indecision and fear played across her face as she stood on the edge, trying to summon her courage to take that downward step. Yet, as much as she desired it, she would often lose her nerve and eventually just sit down and scoot across!

Every day, I am faced with impediments to my spiritual growth—worry, lack of trust, pride, or feelings of hopelessness. I can well understand Faith's reluctance to push through an obstacle that seems insurmountable. I, too, often lack the courage to take the step that would release me from the confines of my fears and bless me with a newfound freedom. Yet, God has assured me of His faithfulness and will never abandon me. He sends me the Holy Spirit to give me the strength and grace to keep moving, even when the obstacle in front of me seems overwhelming.

When I feel weak and lacking in confidence, I need to pull out my spiritual strengtheners—prayer and Scripture. Trust is built by spending time with God in prayer and meditating upon the promises in His Word. The more my confidence in God grows, the greater risks I am willing to take in stepping out in faith. Sometimes I will waver; sometimes I will walk bravely; but I will continue making progress, even if it means I often must sit down and scoot!

[F]or we walk by faith, not by sight. (2 Corinthians 5:7)

Trust in the LORD with all your heart, on your own intelligence do not rely; In all your ways be mindful of him, and he will make straight your paths. (Proverbs 3:5–6)

Childproofing

As Faith became more ambulatory, it was imperative that measures were taken to ensure her protection and well-being. Anti-shock caps were installed in all electrical wall outlets. Cabinets were equipped with childproof locks. Baby gates sprang up, blocking the most vulnerable areas of the house. All outside door handles were covered in safety knobs. Small breakable objects were removed from hands' reach, and guard rails were installed on her toddler bed. Our diligent efforts allowed Faith the freedom to explore her world in safety and contentment.

I am a child in God's eyes. While I see with adult eyes and reason with adult logic, I am still vulnerable to the deceptive tactics of the enemy. Often, I lack the spiritual wisdom necessary to keep me from all harm. But my all-powerful Father watches over me and provides the graces I need to resist temptation and to stay on the path of righteousness. He hems me in, protects me under the shadow of His wings, and covers me in the blood of the cross. He clothes me in spiritual armor to thwart the arrows of the enemy. He stands behind me and whispers, "This way!" And He furnishes me with the shield of faith and the sword of His Word.

Faith was unaware her world was carefully orchestrated to minimize the risks to her welfare. I am not always mindful of the hand of God working in my life, but I can rest assured that He is ever vigilant and ever faithful in His protection of me.

He will rescue you from the fowler's snare, from the destroying plague, He will shelter you with his pinions, and under his wings you may take refuge; his faithfulness is a protecting shield. (Psalm 91:3–4)

[M]y God, my rock of refuge! My shield, my saving horn, my stronghold, my refuge, my savior, from violence you keep me safe. (2 Samuel 22:3)

Whirlwinds

CHILDREN STRUGGLE TO STAY STILL. Faith was no exception. Once she began walking, she was a perpetual whirlwind. Hyperactivity, a condition caused by her prematurity, kept her running from one activity to another. When her little body eventually ran out of steam, she would stop, relax, and immediately fall into a deep sleep. I loved to watch her sleep; it was the only time she was truly calm.

I, too, struggle with hyperactivity, a condition I impose upon myself. My days are filled with constant activity, the need to be productive always driving me to keep going. My mind, swinging from one thought to the next, seems impossible to still. Perhaps the urge to keep moving, both physically and mentally, is my attempt to reign in and tightly control the events and circumstances of my life.

Sitting still, on the other hand, releases those controls and relinquishes the outcomes of life's challenges to my Creator—a feat I can accomplish only through the interaction of the Holy Spirit. Jesus asks me to grow quiet, to loosen my grip on steering the direction of my life, and to allow Him to fight my daily battles.

My mind and body relax only when I acknowledge He is in control. In the stillness of His presence, my soul is restored!

[M]y God, in you I trust. (Psalm 25:2)

My soul, be at rest in God alone, from whom comes my hope. God alone is my rock and my salvation, my fortress; I shall not fall. (Psalm 62:6–7)

Oh My Goodness!

A HOT SUMMER DAY WAS the perfect time to take a ride to the beach. With young Faith in tow, we packed our gear and headed for the Texas Gulf Coast. This trip would be Faith's first encounter with a body of water greater than a plastic blowup swimming pool! As I unbuckled Faith from her car seat upon arrival, I turned her toward the ocean. With eyes as big as saucers, she gasped and exclaimed, "Oh my goodness!" Nothing in her tiny life's experiences had prepared her for the powerful sight of a vast ocean that stretched endlessly in all directions.

Scripture speaks of the vast magnificence of God. Yet, my own limited life's experiences often give me a very narrow view of my Creator. I underestimate the "bigness" of God. Instead, I confine God to the constraints of my finite mind. I box God in by narrowing the scope of my prayers or by expecting God to act in a way that often limits His power.

But God's power and majesty are endless. Where I see limitations, God sees a multitude of possibilities. While my love is conditional, God's love knows no bounds. When I am filled with doubt or unforgiveness, God's mercy and compassion surpass even the heavens.

Priest and author, Richard Rohr, states, "God is always bigger than the boxes we build for God, so we should not waste too much time protecting the boxes." If I can break out of the confines of my own narrow thinking and embrace the vast mystery of God, then perhaps I, too, will be moved to exclaim, "Oh my goodness!"

For my thoughts are not your thoughts, nor are your ways my ways—oracle of the LORD. For as the heavens are higher than the earth, so are my ways higher than your ways, my thoughts higher than your thoughts. (Isaiah 55:8–9)

Oh, the depth of the riches and wisdom and knowledge of God! How inscrutable are his judgments and how unsearchable his ways! (Romans 11:33)

A Child's Love

FAITH LOVED PEOPLE AND WAS everyone's sweetheart. Her bubbly personality, golden curls, and engaging smile made her an instant hit with all who met her. Unsuspecting strangers would get a warm hug around the knees, which invariably elicited "oohs" and "aahs." When someone bent down to greet her, she would throw her arms around their neck and squeeze tight. Her love was irresistible!

Is it possible for me, an adult, to love with such reckless abandon? Can I generously open my heart to those who cross my path and greet them warmly and without prejudice? Scripture states that everyone deserves to be loved, yet it is not always easy to do. The neighbor on the street who refuses to respond to my efforts of friendship, those whose beliefs and customs are at odds with mine, or individuals who trample on the rights of others are especially challenging. Even the unkempt homeless person soliciting on the street corner or the countless others who live outside the margins of society make me uncomfortable.

Unlike Faith, I see the differences in people, and those variances quantify my love. Perhaps I am also stymied by the belief that loving them requires action on my part—an effort to change their situations so that they will become more lovable. Yet, this is not the kind of love that Jesus commands me to do. He asks me to love with a pure heart that does not demand anything in return. The only effort that I am asked to make, according to St. Teresa of Calcutta, is to simply smile. She states, "Let us always meet each other with a smile, for a smile is the beginning of love."

He said to him, "You shall love the LORD, your God, with all your heart, with all your soul, and with all your mind. This is the greatest and the first commandment. The second is like it: You shall love your neighbor as yourself." (Matthew 22:37–39)

This is my commandment: love one another as I love you. (John 15:12)

God of Surprises

WHAT CHILD DOESN'T LOVE SURPRISES? Birthday surprises, hidden goodies in plastic Easter eggs, the contents of a Christmas present, the surprise of a visit from a loved one—all are met with childhood glee! When Faith would find a ladybug, a perfectly formed pinecone, or discover the joys of a new playground, her face would light up as she squealed and giggled with glee! In her innocence, nothing seemed impossible, and all was received in delight.

My God is also a God of surprises. Unlike Faith, though, I set limitations on Him and cannot think beyond the limits of my own intellect. When faced with a problem, I pray for a solution of my own logic, forgetting that with God, all things are feasible. Here is a God who divides the Red Sea, walks on water, and multiplies bread and fish to feed a multitude of people. With this God, possibilities are limitless. While I look at a desert and see only waves of sand, God looks and sees each grain of sand as a possible solution. His thinking is so far above my own thoughts, His ways so superior to my own that I am foolish to even attempt to solve my own problems. It is much more freeing to leave it all to my Creator and allow Him to surprise me with His perfect answer. Every day, I need to adopt the eagerness of a child and proclaim, "Good morning, God. I can't wait to see how you are going to surprise me today!"

Jesus looked at them and said, "For human beings this is impossible, but for God all things are possible." (Matthew 19:26)

I know that you can do all things, and that no purpose of yours can be hindered. (Job 42:2)

Red Lights

WHEN FAITH WAS OLD ENOUGH to recognize her colors, she became fascinated with traffic lights. She knew that when the light was red, we would stop. Eager to see it turn green, she would begin to chant, "Turn gween! Turn gween!" When the red light "obeyed" and changed to green, she was thrilled!

I have always resented having to stop at red lights and stop signs. I want all my lights to be green and wish that I really did have the power to command the light to change from red to green. Red lights interrupt my journey and waste my time. They are a hindrance to accomplishing my overloaded agenda.

But then, a small voice whispers inside of me, "Think of how often Jesus stopped." He stopped to heal the sick and brokenhearted. He stopped to cast out demons and to feed thousands of people. He stopped His desire to be alone to pray and instead got in a boat to preach to the multitudes who followed Him. He took the time to change water into wine, to greet the children, and to wash the feet of His apostles. But most importantly, He stopped His ministry to pick up a cross and carry it up a hill where His life was cruelly ended. The blood that He shed on the cross stopped the gates of hell and guaranteed my salvation.

I stop because the law says I must. Jesus stopped out of His overwhelming love for me.

Jesus stopped and called them and said, "What do you want me to do for you?" (Matthew 20:32)

The way we came to know love was that he laid down his life for us. (1 John 3:16)

Love Hurts

FAITH WAS A CURIOUS, LIVELY child who was fearless in exploring her world. She needed constant supervision to keep her from harming herself. Yet, she still had her share of mishaps—falling headfirst into a small pond, walking through a bed of ants, and constantly scraping her knees on the concrete. Each time she was in trouble, though, I was immediately at her side to rescue her. When Faith hurt, I hurt, and I would do anything to relieve her pain and discomfort.

My LORD is also hurt by my sins and those of all mankind. Do I hurt when He hurts? Would I have felt the same compassion for Him if I had personally witnessed His suffering on His way to Calvary?

What would it have been like to stand and gaze upon this bloodied Jesus? What would it have been like to notice the bruised and cut flesh of His feet that had been dragged over rough terrain by unruly men, knowing that they would be torn even more as

He is pushed down the Via de la Rosa? What would it have been like to see His once white clothing, now muddied, torn, and matted with blood, knowing that this garment would be cruelly ripped from His body, reopening wounds that had yet to heal? What would it have been like to look into His swollen and battered face that had been spat upon, slapped, and ridiculed, knowing that face would be further marred from falling under the weight of a heavy wooden cross? What would I have thought as I followed the trickle of blood oozing from His forehead from the crown of needle-like thorns encircling His head? What would I have felt as I looked deeply into His pain-filled eyes, knowing He was suffering so terribly with more agony yet to come?

It would have felt like falling in love. Looking into those deeply compassionate eyes filled with such unfathomable love for me, His child, would pierce me to the core. He did this for me. This kind of love hurts. This kind of love heals and transforms. This kind of love brings me to my knees in unspeakable gratitude. Through encountering the bloodied Jesus, yes, I am filled with compassion. But more importantly, I am filled with inexplicable joy that in the face of Calvary, I experience redeeming love and am forever changed.

So Jesus came out, wearing the crown of thorns and the purple cloak. And he said to them, "Behold, the man!" (John 19:5)

But he was pierced for our sins, crushed for our iniquity. He bore the punishment that makes us whole, by his wounds we were healed. (Isaiah 53:5)

Hello, Poppie!

THE TELEPHONE HELD A GREAT fascination for Faith. Mimicking others, she would grab the phone, cradle it against her ear, and say "Hello, Poppie, is dat you?" She then proceeded to babble into the phone as if she were actually speaking with her Poppie.

I enjoyed watching Faith's antics with the telephone. It was obvious how much she loved her Poppie and wanted to be in contact with him. I, too, love my heavenly "Poppie" and desire every day to seek Him and converse with Him through prayer. But what is prayer?

St. Thérèse of Lisieux describes prayer as "a lifting of the heart towards God." I can pray anytime during the day simply by placing my focus on Jesus and uttering heartfelt words of praise, thanksgiving, or petition. It doesn't have to be more than a few words. In fact, the less said, the better.

Prayer, like a telephone, is a marvelous tool for maintaining contact with my LORD for every detail of my life. At times, I have been criticized for wasting God's time by praying for mundane things, such as parking places. But I am the apple of Jesus's eye, and there is nothing more He wants than for me to stay in dialogue with Him for all my needs and desires. I can even communicate with my breath, each exhalation representing a sigh of praise for Him.

The scriptures admonish us "to pray without ceasing" (1 Thessalonians 5:17). Stopping throughout my day and sending up tiny arrow prayers straight to the heart of Jesus keeps me connected and helps me more easily recognize the voice of my Savior when I call to say, "Hello."

Have no anxiety at all, but in everything, by prayer and petition, with thanksgiving, make your requests known to God. (Philippians 4:6)

And if we know that he hears us in regard to whatever we ask, we know that what we have asked him for is ours. (1 John 5:15)

Stooping Down

CHILDREN MISBEHAVE, AND FAITH WAS no exception. On the days when she was disobedient or inattentive, it was necessary to correct her with loving authority. I would bend down, look her in the eye, and speak to her about her behavior. Lowering myself to her level focused her attention and conveyed the seriousness of my message. Even words of love and encouragement are better received when a child is eye to eye with the speaker.

Jesus encountered many disobedient and sinful people in His lifetime. None is more striking, however, than the story of the adulterous woman. As she stood before Him while the crowd screamed for her death, Jesus simply knelt and began doodling in the sand. By lowering Himself, Jesus's body language conveyed acceptance, lack of censorship, and humbleness. However, when He addressed her, He rose to a stance of authority, faced her, and spoke, "Go and sin no more" (John 8:11)! Jesus said very few words to this woman; yet, His body language spoke volumes of love and forgiveness.

Jesus disciplines me also. When my actions or thoughts have been displeasing, He does not condemn me. Instead, He stoops to my level, looks me in the eye, and tells me my sins are forgiven. He opens His arms, just as He did on the cross, and receives me in love. As the Reverend Billy Graham stated, "He stoops down to make us great. That's God's grace!"

But you, LORD, take note of me to raise me up. (Psalm 41:11)

Jesus bent down and began to write on the ground with his finger. (John 8:6)

The Holy Chip!

WHENEVER WE TOOK FAITH TO church as a young child, she would protest when she was not allowed to receive Holy Communion. Tearfully, she would complain, "But I wanna get the Holy Chip!"

Huh? I never thought about God being compared to a potato chip! After further reflection, though, I think it fits. God is the bread of life; He is the ideal comfort food; and like potato chips, I am never satisfied with just one piece. I want the whole bag!

Chips come in an assortment of sizes and flavorings. Similarly, my experiences with God have been multi-flavored and unpredictable. Some experiences of Him are sweet and mild while others are surprisingly bold. Yet, the more I encounter God, the more my heart craves Him. St. Augustine recognized this longing for God when he stated, "Our hearts are restless until they rest in you."

My restive spirit longs for God in the sights and sounds of my everyday world where I can fill my senses with the wonder of His beauty. I taste His goodness in the savory words of Scripture, in prayer, and through the frequent reception of the Eucharist. But more importantly, my hungry heart begs to be fed daily with the Holy Spirit whose overwhelming love is so divine!

And God does not disappoint! He says that when we seek Him, we will find Him (Jeremiah 29:13). God Himself has created this deep longing within me which He knows only His presence in my life can help satiate.

Yes, my God is like a bag of potato chips—enjoyable, gratifying, yet always leaving me yearning for more!

*Taste and see that the L*ORD
is good. (Psalm 34:9)

[L]ike newborn infants, long for pure spir-
itual milk so that through it you may
grow into salvation, for you have tasted
*that the L*ORD *is good. (1 Peter 2:2–3)*

My soul yearns for you at night, yes, my spirit
within me seeks you at dawn. (Isaiah 26:9)

The Flowers Need Milk!

IT WAS GARDEN DAY AT the local neighborhood gathering place. A master gardener was presenting information on the flowers and vegetation that would grow well in our area. As Faith and I listened to the presenter and observed the flowers that were growing in the sample bed, Faith suddenly jumped off my lap, toddled over to the presenter's side, and announced in her most commanding voice, "These flowers need a drink! They need milk!"

How often do I try to tell God what I need to solve my life's issues? Frequently, I forget that God is the expert who knows exactly what nutrients are necessary for me to reap the greatest rewards. Instead, I foolishly try to intervene, offering God advice, and insisting He furnish me with what I believe is the perfect solution for all my needs. Patiently and gently, He shows me that my way is not necessarily the best path for my healing and growth.

St. Paul teaches that when we are children, we think, act, and reason as a child (1 Corinthians 13:11). But as an adult, I am encouraged to put aside my childish ideas and to place my trust solely in the Master Gardner who is expertly in charge of the gardening of my soul.

Your heavenly Father knows that you need them all. But seek first the kingdom [of God] and his righteousness, and all these things will be given you besides. (Matthew 6:32–33)

Moreover, God is able to make every grace abundant for you, so that in all things, always having all you need, you may have an abundance for every good work. (2 Corinthians 9:8)

Refrigerator Pictures

FAITH WAS HIGHLY CREATIVE. SHE loved finger painting, sculpting with Play-Doh, or drawing on her pad of paper. Many of her creations adorned our refrigerator—her proud gifts of herself to us.

Jesus also enjoys creating, and I am one of His most valued masterpieces. He cannot get enough of me. He is always tweaking me, shaping this part, molding this area, sanding off my rough edges. It is like having a hobby on steroids! My favorite hobby is decorative painting. Sometimes I become so enamored with a piece I am creating that I am reluctant to finish it. I keep embellishing—a stronger color here, another stroke there, sometimes adding adornments like glitter dust or decorative stones. When I fall in love with a piece, I cannot leave it alone.

Likewise, Jesus does not want to let go of me. I am His favorite hobby. He loves what He has created; yet, He never tires of painting my soul with more grace, more love, more intimacy with Him. He is continually transforming me into His perfect image and will do so until the end of time. I am His special work of art, and He delights in me. Open the palm of His hand, and you will find my image. Enter the door of His heavenly home and discover my picture hanging on His wall. Just as Faith's scribbled drawings were priceless to us, so, too, does God treasure His creation of me.

Yet, LORD, you are our father; we are the clay and you our potter: we are all the work of your hand. (Isaiah 64:7)

For we are his handiwork, created in Christ Jesus for the good works that God has prepared in advance, that we should live in them. (Ephesians 2:10)

All of us, gazing with unveiled face on the glory of the LORD, are being transformed into the same image from glory to glory, as from the LORD who is the Spirit. (2 Corinthians 3:18)

I Found Me!

"POPPIE," THREE-YEAR-OLD FAITH INSTRUCTED WHILE playing hide and seek with her grandfather, "You count, and I'll hide." Following her instructions, Poppie began to count. Just as he shouted, "Here I come, ready or not," Faith came running back into the room, threw open her arms, and gleefully exclaimed, "I found me!"

While Faith may not have understood the rules of the game of hide and seek, her response clearly echoes my desire to "find" myself. But to find myself, I must first find God. As I travel my spiritual path, seeking God, I need to remember that He is actively traveling toward me!

God not only wants me to seek Him, but He desperately wants to find me. Shawn McCarty, in his book, *Partners in the Divine Dance*, states, "It may be more proper to say that in our search for God, God finds us more than we find God." God seeks me out in the quiet recesses of my heart, in the minutia of my every-day life, in my doubts, fears, joys, successes and failures, in my relationships with others, and more importantly, in my time of prayer and solitude with Him. At these times, He not only reveals Himself to me, but He also reveals who I am—His cherished child. My good shepherd seeks me out just as He sought out the one lost sheep, and He will not rest until I am found!

*Draw near to God, and he will
draw near to you. (James 4:8)*

*Yet when you seek the L*ORD*, your God,
from there, you shall indeed find him
if you search after him with all your
heart and soul. (Deuteronomy 4:29)*

*The L*ORD *is good to those who trust in him, to
the one that seeks him; (Lamentations 3:25)*

Rock Star

AT A PRESCHOOL PROGRAM, THE children were asked what they wanted to be when they grew up. Faith approached the microphone, giggled, and loudly proclaimed, "I want to be a rock star!" Of course, she had no idea what being a rock star entailed. It just seemed glamorous and fun—a profession that would allow her to bask in the spotlight.

I also find myself asking, "What am I doing with my life? What legacy do I want to leave behind that marks my life as a life well lived?" While I do not seek fame and glamour, I do seek holiness. Holiness is striving for a greater intimacy with God and allowing His grace to chip away at any obstacles that prevent His light from shining through me. It is being obedient to His will and trusting in His divine providence. As St. Thérèse of Lisieux states, "We become holy by doing the little things."

Gathering holiness through simple acts of kindness, compassion, and a prayerful approach to everyday life will increase the sacredness within and allow the goodness of God to take center stage. It is my desire, therefore, that holiness will give my life purpose and value and assure me of a place in God's kingdom. Then, as I approach His heavenly throne, God will smile and proudly proclaim, "Here comes my rock star!"

Strive for peace with everyone, and for that holiness without which no one will see the LORD. (Hebrews 12:14)

[B]ut, as he who called you is holy, be holy yourselves in every aspect of your conduct, for it is written, "Be holy because I [am] holy." (1 Peter 1:15–16)

"Utterflies"

EVEN THOUGH FAITH HAD A rough beginning, she developed into a happy, healthy little girl who had such a zest for life. She loved to go "owside" and explore nature's gifts. For her "utterflies" were magnificent, leaves were souvenirs to be collected, and "bootiful" flowers were to be smelled, picked, tasted, and shared. There was nothing more delightful to her than the sights, textures, and sounds of the outdoors.

What makes a child look upon her world with such wide-eyed wonder and love? Perhaps as a new creature, a toddler still carries the memories of the joy of being with God in creation. As I age, my memory of heavenly things fades, and I become indifferent to the colors, sights, and sounds of my natural world. Now it takes a concentrated effort to stop my daily activities, step outside, and marvel at the wonders around me—the formation of the clouds, the vast expanse of a starry night sky, the intricate structure of a leaf, a rock, or even a roly-poly bug! My frenetic-paced life robs me of the ability to stop and observe my surroundings with curiosity and reverence.

And yet, God did not create my world in such perfect detail so that I could rush by and miss the healing that comes from breathing in and experiencing its beauty. Nature gives me the freedom to let go, to fill my senses, and to add balance to my life. My natural environment is a window into the divine presence of God and draws me more fully into communion with Him. All around me is a miracle! I only need to observe my world with the eyes of a child to appreciate how "bootiful" it truly is.

God looked at everything he had made,
and found it very good. (Genesis 1:31)

The heavens declare the glory of God,
the firmament proclaims the works
of his hands. (Psalm 19:2)

Worn-Out Tummies

AFTER SUFFERING FOR SEVERAL DAYS with a stomach bug, Faith slowly walked halfway down the stairs, plopped down, and wearily exclaimed, "I can't make it! My tummy is just wearing me out!" How well I understand Faith's lament! Sometimes painful events in my life just wear me out too!

When a particularly troublesome issue presents itself, I wrestle and struggle with the problem. I plan, scheme, fret, and drain myself trying to find a solution. I plead my case before the LORD and incessantly beg for an end to my suffering. Only when exhausted can I grow quiet enough to hear the small soft voice of the LORD saying, "Let go." Such a simple idea, but such a challenging feat to put into practice!

It is difficult to abandon my own desires in surrender to His will. It is even harder to say, "Have your way, LORD." Yet, there is freedom in letting go, in allowing God free rein to bring about the best plan for my welfare. His plan is so superior to my own agenda. His thoughts are so far above my thoughts; His ways so above my ways (Isaiah 55:8–9). God never fails to meet my needs, often in surprising ways.

My God of surprises can do infinitely more than I can humanly imagine if I will let down my defenses, raise my hands, and whisper, "I surrender!" What power those two words unleash! They are the miraculous cure that transforms my worries into anticipation, my anticipation into hope, and my hope into reaped blessings!

Humble yourselves before the LORD and he will exalt you. (James 4:10)

Cast all your worries upon him because he cares for you. (1 Peter 5:7)

Beach Time

IT WAS A HOT SUNNY day at the beach. Faith ran excitedly from the beach to the water's edge, squealing every time a wave threatened to approach her. Still very tentative around the power of the ocean, she stayed close to shore but eventually was persuaded to wade into the water with the promise that I would be right beside her.

Looking around at the other beachgoers, I was struck by how differently people reacted to the lure of the ocean. Some sat contently in their beach chairs, enjoying the sights, sounds, and smells of the ocean, but refusing to venture into the water. Others tentatively waded in a few feet, never going more than ankle deep. Still, there were those who would plunge right in—some headfirst, some on surfboards, others enthusiastically jumping and frolicking in the waves. These adventuresome souls were the ones who refused to play it safe, refused even to go halfway. Instead, they accepted the full challenge of swimming in the ocean, soaking themselves from head to toe, and paying little attention to what others thought as they squealed and laughed in delight.

What a metaphor for my life and my willingness to trust in my God! Too often I play it safe, fearful of venturing out of my spiritual comfort zone. Sometimes I do take a risk in trusting God, but only to the ankle-deep level. It is difficult to have the courage to completely let go and to dive right into God's infinite love and allow the waves of that love to take me to greater heights and deeper depths in my spiritual growth. Yet, there is freedom and joy in relinquishing the control of my life and trusting in His promise to always keep me safe. My desire is that I can eventually gain enough courage, as Faith did, to plunge into the waters of God's perfect will and simply enjoy the pleasures of His oceanic love!

There is no fear in love, but perfect love drives out fear because fear has to do with punishment, and so one who fears is not yet perfect in love. (1 John 4:18)

Be strong, all you people of the land—oracle of the LORD—and work! For I am with you—oracle of the LORD of hosts. (Haggai 2:4)

Itsy-Bitsy Spider

IT WAS THE FIRST DAY of the celebration of the annual Livestock and Rodeo show. The convention center was full of vendors selling wares of every conceivable kind. As we walked the aisles, two-year-old Faith seemed unimpressed until she spotted a merchant selling water softeners. Cleverly, the vendor had used a wall of cascading water as his backdrop. Faith immediately let go of my hand, ran into the booth, stood in front of the waterfall, and began to sing at the top of her lungs, "Itsy-bitsy spider went up the waterspout!" Everyone within earshot stopped and watched this miniature star perform her solo.

I marveled at this child's innocence and complete lack of self-consciousness as she belted out her song. Her pleasure was contagious. How often have I wished that I could be that bold in proclaiming the joys of my faith? Saying grace in restaurants before a meal; offering to pray for a stranger who seemed in need; saying "God bless you" to the grocery clerk—all take a humbleness and lack of concern of what others may think.

Jesus Himself was bold in His proclamation of the Gospel. He sought out sinners, lepers, and beggars and offered them words of hope and healing, despite the criticisms and abuse of the unbelievers. With the help of my God and the example of a two-year-old, perhaps I, too, can learn to be confident in proclaiming the good works of the LORD through my words and actions.

He said to them, "Go into the whole world and proclaim the Gospel to every creature." (Mark 16:15)

Therefore, do not throw away your confidence; it will have great recompense. (Hebrews 10:35)

Monsters Under the Bed

As FAITH GREW AND BECAME more aware of her surroundings, she developed a fear of the dark. She insisted on having a light at bedtime that would remain on throughout the night. A night-light was not enough—it had to be brighter before she felt relaxed enough to fall asleep.

I can well understand a child's fear of the dark. Even as an adult, I still find myself uncomfortable when I am alone and all the lights are out. My rational brain tells me that I am safe, but my emotional response is that of a child who sees monsters under the bed.

Darkness in my spiritual life can have the same effect. When difficulties occur and the light of the Spirit dims, I, too, feel afraid and anxious. I become despondent and bewildered by the sense that God has abandoned me in my time of need. Yet, it is the darkness that triggers the greatest spiritual growth.

Mother Angelica, founder of EWTN, says it this way: "The darkness of faith is just as pleasing to God as the consolations of faith. In fact, the darkness of faith is what prunes you, detaches you, and makes you love God with a pure love."

When I am in desolation and all that is familiar is obscured, my need for God becomes even more pressing. God is my source of light, and His flame burning inside of me is stronger than any darkness. By fanning that small spark with faith and trust in Him, that flame grows and illuminates all the hidden recesses of my heart that need to be healed or swept clean. The light provides me greater clarity and understanding of my relationship with my Creator.

Throughout my spiritual journey, the dark times of the soul will wane and appear as surely as the rising and setting of the sun. However, the dark is not to be feared. Rather, it is in darkness that I can grow in greater intimacy with my Creator. It is in the dark that I can fall more deeply in love.

You are my lamp, O LORD! My God brightens the darkness about me. (2 Samuel 22:29)

[T]he light shines in the darkness, and the darkness has not overcome it. (John 1:5)

Hiccups

AFTER BEING TREATED FOR A bronchial infection, Faith became very enamored with medication. Long after she recovered and no longer needed treatment, she would ask for a dose of medicine for every real or imaginary discomfort she experienced. One day, she informed me she needed some medicine because she was "berry" sick.

"What's wrong?" I asked her.

"I've got the hiccups!" she announced.

Hiccups are annoying. On the rare occasion when I experience them, I will hold my breath, drink water, and try various methods to alleviate them. But hiccups are a part of life. Any event in my daily routine that is out of sync, troublesome, or anxiety ridden is a hiccup that has the potential to derail me from my trust and faith in God. Sometimes these glitches in life eventually even out without too much disruption. Other times, it takes a strong dose of prayer, praise, and blind obedience to weather the unease of a situation. Part of the anxiety comes from believing that these interruptions in life will never cease. Mother Angelica points out in her writings, "Our worry comes from making impermanent things seem permanent."

I will always have hiccups in my life; but if I wait upon the LORD, acknowledge His supremacy over every detail of my world, and trust in His love and wisdom, my life's ups and downs will only lead to grace and growth.

Worry weighs down the heart, but a kind word gives it joy. (Proverbs 12:25)

Can any of you by worrying add a moment to your life span? If even the smallest things are beyond your control, why are you anxious about the rest? (Luke 12:25–26)

Chocolate "Maters"

EVEN AS A YOUNG CHILD, Faith loved tomatoes. If allowed, she would have gladly devoured them at every meal. As we shopped for groceries one day, Faith had her sights out for her favorite food. Spying a bin of ripe avocados, she excitedly exclaimed, "Look, Grammie, chocolate maters!"

I laughed at Faith's innocent mistake, but then I realized how easy it is to mislabel the events of my life while God perceives a different reality. I see trials as suffering to be avoided. God sees trials as loving discipline, opportunities for grace, and an invitation to share in the passion of His Son. I see disappointments as setbacks in life; God sees them as periods of growth. When I am sinful, I see myself as unworthy of God's mercy and forgiveness. God observes me through a lens of love and welcomes me into His warm embrace where all is forgiven and forgotten. When I am hard on myself for my weaknesses, God sees my perfection in Him. When I feel lost and confused, God foresees the perfect plan for my life and gives me the grace to trust in His wisdom. My knowledge is limited, yet the Word cautions me to not rely upon my own intelligence (Proverbs 3:5). God perceives all, knows all, and loves all. He sees *all* the fruit of my life while I may only see tomatoes!

For I know well the plans I have in mind for you—oracle of the LORD—plans for your welfare and not for woe, so as to give you a future of hope. (Jeremiah 29:11)

In this you rejoice, although now for a little while you may have to suffer through various trials, so that the genuineness of your faith, more precious than gold that is perishable even though tested by fire, may prove to be for praise, glory, and honor at the revelation of Jesus Christ. (1 Peter 1:6–7)

Run, Grammie, Run

AFTER LEARNING TO WALK, FAITH almost immediately began to run. Running was her favorite mode of transportation! It was difficult to keep up with her. I was always trailing behind as she raced ahead, frequently turning her head to yell, "Run, Grammie, Run!"

I do not like to run; it makes my chest hurt. A brisk walk is more my pace. However, there are times in my life when I need to run. When I am feeling discouraged and carrying a backpack of worries, I need to run to the Scriptures and feed on words of hope and encouragement. When my body aches or is ill, I must run to the God of healing and mercy. When I feel dry and my prayers are brittle, I should hurry to the feet of my Father and remain there until the desolation passes. When I am frightened and anxiety threatens to overcome me, I must run to my Father, climb up on His lap, and let His arms encircle me with love and protection. When I feel disgruntled, I need to race toward gratitude for a God who blesses me tremendously and is always faithful to me.

Running is especially necessary when I have sinned against my Father. At those times, I must sprint as fast as I can to the foot of the cross where the blood of the crucified Jesus washes me clean. Even during times of spiritual consolation, I should never stop running to my amazing God who shares in my joys and accomplishments.

My body will never enjoy the act of running physically; but if I want to grow spiritually in strength and stamina, running to my Father must always be a part of my daily exercise.

Therefore, since we are surrounded by so great a cloud of witnesses, let us rid ourselves of every burden and sin that clings to us and persevere in running the race that lies before us. (Hebrews 12:1)

*They that hope in the L*ORD *will renew their strength, they will soar on eagles' wings; They will run and not grow weary, walk and not grow faint. (Isaiah 40:31)*

Equipped for the Task

FAITH LOVED TO BE A helper. If I grabbed a broom to sweep, she had to have her own child-sized broom and dustpan to work beside me. When I donned my apron to cook, Faith would put on her small apron, climb up on a stool, and ask to help. If I gardened, she would have her gloves and child's shovel to help weed or plant. Whatever needed to be done, Faith would be fitted with her own miniature equipment so that she could easily handle the task at hand.

In God's eyes, when faced with a task, I too need to be equipped to be able to perform without handicap. Therefore, He does not burden me with more than I can handle. Scripture tells me that He takes the greater load upon himself and leaves me with a lighter yoke (Matthew 11:30). Too often, though, I immediately place my focus on my own limitations and weaknesses. I judge that my faith is not strong enough, my courage weak, and my gifts lacking. Yet, throughout both the Old and New Testament, God called not the strong but the weak to fulfill His purpose. Moses stuttered; Abraham was aged; the apostles were uneducated fishermen or greedy tax collectors. But through their unshakable trust and belief in God, they were used by God and are forever remembered for their mighty deeds.

What a relief to realize that my limitations are not a hindrance but a conduit for God's glory to shine through! My confidence soars as I grasp the truth that in striving to do His will, He will provide all the necessary tools and graces that are sized just for my success. As British evangelist Smith Wigglesworth stated, "God does not call those who are equipped. He equips those whom He has called."

May the God of peace, who brought up from the dead the great shepherd of the sheep by the blood of the eternal covenant, Jesus our LORD, *furnish you with all that is good, that you may do his will. May he carry out in you what is pleasing to him through Jesus Christ, to whom be glory forever [and ever]. Amen. (Hebrews 13:20–21)*

My God will fully supply whatever you need, in accord with his glorious riches in Christ Jesus. (Philippians 4:19)

Band-Aids

FAITH WAS CRAZY ABOUT BAND-AIDS. Every hurt, imaginary or real, could only be fixed with a Band-Aid. She would have gladly covered her whole body with those colorful fairy princess strips if allowed. For her, Band-Aids were the only way to treat her boo-boos.

I, too, like Band-Aids—not the physical kind that sticks to my skin, but the spiritual ones that provide a quick fix for whatever is ailing me. When I encounter a difficulty, a pain, a woundedness, I want God to remedy it with an easy solution—a tiny sliver of grace that will provide instant healing. But some wounds are too big for a Band-Aid. Some wounds go deep and require extensive healing treatments to provide relief. And there are other wounds that should never be covered, but should be allowed to be open, to even bleed for healing to take place. This is not my preferred method of treatment, but as a cancer survivor, I know firsthand that suffering sometimes requires more than a quick fix.

Suffering is difficult, not easily understood, and not always eliminated by the methods of my choice. But suffering is not without grace. Every time I suffer, I am privileged to take part in the suffering of God's Son. I am given the opportunity to surrender to Him in complete faith and trust. It is through suffering that I come to see another face of God—the face of fidelity and compassion. My relationship with Him is strengthened, and my ability to allow God to be God is stretched.

I will always want a quick Band-Aid to cover my hurts. But when greater measures are required, I pray and believe that God will cover me with grace and lovingly restore me to wholeness.

Blessed is the man who perseveres in temptation, for when he has been proved he will receive the crown of life that he promised to those who love him. (James 1:12)

For as Christ's sufferings overflow to us, so through Christ does our encouragement also overflow. (2 Corinthians 1:5)

Secrets

AS A CHILD, IT WAS always fun to play the game "Secrets" where we would tell a deep dark secret and then pinky swear never to reveal it. Faith told me a secret one day. She whispered, "I know where you hide the M&M's!"

Do I have secrets? Do I keep things sequestered away in my heart that I dare not reveal to anyone, not even my God? Am I always truthful to God about how I really feel about my life's situations? Even in my relationship with others, I wear a face of Christian piety and keep well under wraps any feelings of anger, despair, or helplessness.

Yet, God calls me to be my authentic self with others as well as with Him. My prayers to Him do not need to be cloaked in religious piety or said with a stiff upper lip. Sometimes, the only genuine prayers I can offer to God are prayers of helplessness, prayers of illness, prayers of despair and suffering. At those times, God will remind me that His own Son offered up such prayers. As He hung dying on a cross, Jesus's last act as a human being was to utter the prayer of suffering "My God, My God, why have you forsaken me" (Mark 15:34)? These words were His ultimate supplication from which came the ultimate reward— our salvation.

When I keep no secrets from God, when I lay out all my feelings in their tattered forms, I can taste the reality of His overwhelming love. As I come before the Father in my vulnerability and nakedness, He will take me gently in His arms and whisper a secret: "You are my beloved child."

Stop lying to one another, since you have taken off the old self with its practices and have put on the new self, which is being renewed, for knowledge, in the image of its creator. (Colossians 3:9–10)

Therefore, putting away falsehood, speak the truth, each one to his neighbor, for we are members one of another. (Ephesians 4:25)

The mouth of the just is a fountain of life, but the mouth of the wicked conceals violence. (Proverbs 10:11)

Chasing Laser Beams

FAITH'S DAD HAD A LASER beam that he clicked on and off around the room. Little Faith was mesmerized by that tiny circle of light that seemed to magically appear and disappear. She scrambled from one side of the room to the other trying to catch it. Even though her attempts were fruitless, she never stopped her efforts to grab that elusive red dot!

Happiness is like a laser beam. It is fleeting, mysteriously appearing and disappearing, and always leaves me searching for the next possession, event, or relationship that will make me happy. But God does not promise me happiness. Rather, He invites me to share in His joy.

Joy is a strong word, an emotion that I find more difficult to feel than sorrow. Unlike happiness, joy is not simply a transitory feeling or a brief sentiment; it is a deep-seated result of my connection to God. It is a serene peace that comes from recognizing and embracing God's love and presence in my life. Even in the midst of tragedy, joy is possible. Author Fr. James Martin explains that "finding joy during times of pain begins with the understanding that joy depends not on our circumstances, but on our faith, hope and confidence in God." Joy is not the absence of sadness, but it is the discovery of my connectivity with God amid my pain.

The scriptures are full of examples of joy. One of my favorite Gospel stories describes the joy of Peter while he was out fishing. Looking about, he suddenly realized that the risen Jesus was standing on the shore! In his exuberance, he jumped into the water and swam to Jesus! You might say he jumped into joy! I, too, want to experience that same joy. I want to throw aside my serious, pious Christian demeanor and laugh, dance, and celebrate with enthusiasm my relationship with God. I want to catch and hold that laser beam of joy as a testimony that God is forever present with me!

May the God of hope fill you with all joy and peace in believing, so that you may abound in hope by the power of the holy Spirit. (Romans 15:13)

Do not be saddened this day, for rejoicing in the LORD is your strength! (Nehemiah 8:10)

Let the faithful rejoice in their glory, cry out for joy on their couches. (Psalm 149:5)

Aching Heart

ONCE FAITH WAS OLD ENOUGH, she entered day care. Gone were the days when we could hold and care for her on a routine basis. When time would pass without seeing her, I would experience a physical ache and deep longing for her. Consequently, I would arrange my schedule for a visit. It was only after spending quality time with her that I would once again feel contented.

Is this what Jesus feels for me? Does He ache for me? St. Teresa of Calcutta states that Jesus not only desires our companionship, but "He thirsts for our love."

While on the cross, Jesus exclaimed, "I thirst" (John 19:28). His anguish went beyond the physical need for water, but in those words, He proclaims His thirst for each of us. He longs for us, and nothing delights Him more than to spend time with us in prayer.

I thirst for Him, too, but so often, I allow my busyness to steal away precious moments to be spent with Him. Yet, God waits patiently for me every day to enter His presence and sit with Him. It is as if He reclines in a big armchair across from me and allows me to be His total focus. Our time together can be filled with words or we can simply rest in silence, cocooned in our love for one another.

God desires a relationship with me, not occasionally, but on a day-to-day basis. It does not matter what we do, only that I take the time to drink Him in so that both our thirsts can be satisfied.

For the LORD takes delight in his people.
(Psalm 149:4)

Truly, the LORD is waiting to be gracious to
you, truly, he shall rise to show you mercy;
For the LORD is a God of justice: happy are
all who wait for him! (Isaiah 30:18)

As the deer longs for streams of water, so my
soul longs for you, O God. My soul thirsts
for God, the living God. When can I enter
and see the face of God? (Psalm 42:2–3)

Called by Name

IT WAS FITTING FOR FAITH to be given her name. It took an abundance of faith to believe that she would survive the difficulties resulting from her premature birth. It took more faith to believe that as she grew, she would carry none of the complications that could arise from such an early delivery. She has proven to be the product of a strong belief in the goodness of God and intercessory prayer. She is called Faith, and I believe she is called for a purpose.

We all are called by name by our God. He knows us intimately and has breathed a unique purpose into our lives. Frequently, I have asked God, "What is my purpose?" I long to follow Jesus and to be open to fulfilling His will for my life.

When I hear Jesus's invitation to "come" as He said to Peter who wanted to walk to Him on the water (Matthew 14:29), I want to respond with the same eagerness and enthusiasm. But is jumping in the water as Peter did the only way I can respond to Jesus's calling? Maybe not.

I believe that I have my own unique mission, and the way I fulfill my purpose will not be the same as everyone else's. If all the apostles had jumped into the water, who would have steered the boat? If no one were onboard, who would have hauled Jesus and Peter out of the water? Perhaps another disciple's role was to stay behind to provide reassurance and comfort to the petrified apostles. Each was called to a different, yet equally meaningful, way to fulfill God's will for their lives.

Whether I jump, stay onboard, or even remain on land is dependent on my personal calling and the guidance of the Holy Spirit who calls me by name and simply invites me to "come."

Only, everyone should live as the Lord has assigned, just as God called each one. I give this order in all the churches. (1 Corinthians 7:17)

To this end, we always pray for you, that our God may make you worthy of his calling and powerfully bring to fulfillment every good purpose and every effort of faith. (2 Thessalonians 1:11)

Scripture Index

2 Samuel 22:3
2 Thessalonians 1:11
Colossians 3:9–10
Deuteronomy 28:12
Deuteronomy 4:29
Ecclesiastes 3:1,4
Ephesians 2:10
Ephesians 4:25
Ephesians 6:16
Exodus 20:3
Ezekiel 34:11
Genesis 1:31
Haggai 2:4
Hebrews 10:35
Hebrews 12:1
Hebrews 12:14
Hebrews 12:2
Hebrews 13:20–21
Isaiah 4:6
Isaiah 26:9
Isaiah 30:18
Isaiah 30:21
Isaiah 35:1–2
Isaiah 40:31
Isaiah 53:5
Isaiah 54:17

Isaiah 55:8–9
Isaiah 58:11
Isaiah 61:10
Isaiah 64:7
James 1:12
James 4:8
James 4:10
James 4:12
Jeremiah 1:5
Jeremiah 17:7
Jeremiah 29:11
Job 42:2
John 1:5
John 6:63
John 8:6
John 10:11
John 15:12
John 19:5
Lamentations 3:25
Luke 1:78–79
Luke 12:25–26
Malachi 3:10
Mark 11:24
Mark 16:15
Matthew 2:9
Matthew 6:32

Mathew 11:15
Matthew 16:19
Matthew 19:26
Matthew 20:32
Matthew 22:37–39
Nehemiah 8:10
Philippians 3:7
Philippians 4:9
Philippians 4:19
Proverbs 1:5
Proverbs 3:3–4
Proverbs 3:5–6
Proverbs 10:11
Proverbs 12:25
Psalm 19:2
Psalm 19:15
Psalm 25:2
Psalm 27:4
Psalm 30:12
Psalm 34:9
Psalm 37:5
Psalm 41:11
Psalm 42:2–3
Psalm 46:11
Psalm 51:12
Psalm 56:4

Psalm 62:6–7
Psalm 91:3–4
Psalm 121:3
Psalm 131:2
Psalm 149:4
Psalm 149:5
Romans 5:3–4
Romans 5:8
Romans 8:38–39
Romans 11:33
Romans 15:13
Wisdom 11:23

About the Author

SANDRA SMITH IS A RETIRED teacher who has taught pre-school through adult education. She is an active retreat presenter and spiritual director with the Emmaus Spirituality Center in Houston, Texas. She has served in various leadership roles, including national president of Theresians International, Inc., a faith-based women's global organization. Sandra and husband, Mark, reside in Sugar Land, Texas.